# CORNWA
# HISTO

## PHILIP PAYTON

# Tor Mark

Published by Tor Mark,
United Downs Industrial Estate,
St Day, Redruth, Cornwall TR16 5HY

www.tormark.co.uk

First published 2002, reprinted 2013
This edition 2020

ISBN 978 0 85025 449 5

Printed and bound in Great Britain
by Cambrian Printers

St Michael's Mount

© Werner Wilmes

# INTRODUCTION

© Gwennap Pit

In 1602 Richard Carew in his famous **Survey of Cornwall** wrote that 'Cornwall, as an entire state, hath at divers times enjoyed sundry titles: of a kingdom, principality, duchy, and earldom'. In the same book he added that the Cornish were still 'fostering a fresh memory of their expulsion long ago by the English' and that the over-inquisitive visitor from over the River Tamar border might be rebuffed by the Cornish-language retort **'meea navidna cowza-sawzneck'** – 'I will not speak English'.

Today, the holidaymaker venturing westwards will be met more kindly but he or she will be left in no doubt that Cornwall remains a land apart, and that he or she has left England far behind. Placenames such as Crows-an-wra, Praze-an-Beeble and Trewar-menna betray their Celtic origins, echoing those of Wales and Brittany, while the Cornish language itself may still be heard – kept alive by a small but growing band of dedicated enthusiasts. The black-and-white banner of St Piran, the Cornish flag, is everywhere in evidence, proclaiming Cornwall as the land of 'difference', and if the Cornish rugby team happens to be playing in the County Championships 'Trelawny's Army' will be out in force – thousands of passionate supporters all dressed alike in Cornwall's distinctive black-and-gold jerseys.

But why is Cornwall so 'different'? The answer lies in its history, the story of a people whose separate identity was formed in early times and has weathered centuries of turmoil and change to the present day, constantly 're-inventing' itself from one age to the next. No less than the Welsh or the Scots, the Cornish are one of the constituent peoples of contemporary Britain.

# EARLY
# HISTORY

Cornwall emerges from the murk of prehistory courtesy of Classical writers such Strabo, who mentions a visit by the Roman official Publius Crassus who in the 1st century BC visited the **Cassiterides** (the Tin Isles), modern day Cornwall and Scilly, to organise tin trading with the Mediterranean.

Diodorus, another such writer, thought the inhabitants of the peninsula of Belerion (Cornwall) remarkably sophisticated and civilised, the result of their extensive trading contacts with peoples from other lands. Diodorus explained how the natives of Belerion extracted tin from the ground and then broke it up and smelted it, producing ingots which were taken to the off-shore island of Ictis. Ictis served as a trading post, the place where merchants from the Mediterranean and perhaps elsewhere would come to buy the tin they needed for their domestic markets. Many people think that Ictis is present-day St Michael's Mount but others have suggested St George's (or Looe) Island, further east along the south Cornish coast.

By this time Cornwall was Celtic-speaking, using a variant of a tongue which had emerged in continental Europe during the first millennium BC or thereabouts. Known to scholars as Brythonic or 'British', this variant was the forunner of modern Cornish as well as Welsh and Breton.

How, why and when Celtic became the language of Cornwall is a matter of some conjecture. The old idea that ancient times consisted of a series of mass invasions, with waves of newcomers arriving suddenly to expel or exterminate the existing populations is now open to doubt. Instead, historians now argue that these 'invasions' involved relatively few people who, because of their superior technologies or military prowess, were able to impose their ways (including language) upon the indigenous natives. The Celtic settlement of Britain as a whole is now thought to have been a long, drawn-out affair, perhaps starting early in the first millennium BC and ending with the arrival of the Belgic people not long before the coming of the Romans.

Certainly, the evidence of Iron Age Cornwall is of continuity rather than upheaval, the arrival of Celtic speech coinciding with the first use of iron for weapons and other artifacts. By the time the Romans came to Britain in AD43, the famous promontory and hill forts of Cornwall – Chun Castle, Warbstow Bury, the Rumps, the Dodman, and so on – had already existed for centuries, and some remained occupied (though not continuously) until as late as the 6th century AD. In the west of Cornwall, people were already living in so-called courtyard houses, of which several well known examples survive today. Chysauster, near Gulval, dates from the Roman era but Carn Euny (in the parish of Sancreed) is older, consisting of three interlocking courtyard houses and a remarkable underground chamber or fogou – from the Cornish-language word for 'cave'. These fogous are now thought to have been underground storage larders, although other theories suggest they may have had religious significance or were perhaps hiding-places in case of attack.

The Romans built a fort at **Isca Dumnoniorum** (modern Exeter) in about AD55, and it was from there that they exercised their rule in the far west. In fact, there is very little evidence of Roman intrusion or activity in Cornwall. A small fort, probably used as a forward operating base rather than a garrison, was constructed around AD55-60 at Nanstallon, near Bodmin, and five Roman milestones have been found in different parts of Cornwall. At Carvossa, a large enclosed site near Probus, imported Roman pottery has been found, and the remains of a Romano-British villa have been uncovered at Magor, Illogan. Politically, it seems that Cornwall formed a **pagus** or subdivision of the Roman canton of **Dumnonia** (present-day Cornwall, Devon and western Somerset) but was very much left to its own devices.

Mên-an-Tol

# THE POST-ROMAN PERIOD
# AND THE 'DARK AGES'

When the last of the legions left Britain in about AD 410, Dumnonia survived in name as a post-Roman Celtic kingdom but the reality (or so it seems) was increasing political and territorial fragmentation in the South West peninsula. Certainly, by the 9th century Anglo-Saxon sources were referring to **Cornwalas** or **Westwalas**, while texts in Latin spoke of **Cornubia** and Old Welsh had coined the word **Cerniu** – each of these referring to the kingdom of Kernow or Cornwall, the land of the 'West Welsh', as it had by then become.

It is no longer fashionable to describe the post-Roman era in Britain as 'the Dark Ages' but it is nonetheless a murky period in Cornish history. Half-legendary figures such as Cynan (or Conan) Meriadoc and King Mark appear tantalisingly from the mists, the latter entwined intimately in the tragic tale of Tristan and Iseult. Ultimately a European medieval high romance, taken to France and beyond by way of Brittany, the story of the ill-fated lovers, Tristan and Iseult, has its roots in Dark Age Cornwall.

Near Fowey stands the so-called Tristan Stone, carved with the inscription DRUSTANVS HIC IACIT/CVNOMORI FILIVS – 'Drustanus lies here, son of Cunomorus'. Drustanus has been indentified with the legendary Tristan, and Cunomorus has been equated with the 6th century Marcus Cunomorus ('King Mark') whose fortress is said to be neighbouring Castle Dore.

In the several versions of the story that have come down to us, Tristan is the nephew (not son) of King Mark and is sent to Ireland to seek the hand of Iseult, the Queen's daughter, for Mark. The Queen accepts, and the princess and her maiden Brangwayn set out on their journey to Cornwall. The Queen has given Brangwayn a special love-potion which Iseult and Mark are to drink on their wedding night but by mistake (or design) it is Tristan who sups the magic liquid. Inevitably, Tristan and Iseult fall hopelessly in love, and in the court of King Mark resort to a variety of deceptions to be together. Eventually, Tristan leaves Cornwall to fight for King Hywel of Brittany, where he meets and marries a second Iseult (Iseult of the White Hands). However, the first Iseult begs Tristan to return, and he does so, only to be slain by the angry and jealous King Mark who has uncovered the truth of the liaison.

Mark's son Constantine is described by Gildas about AD560 in his **De Excidio et Conquestu Britanniae** as the 'tyrant whelp of the filthy lioness of Dumnonia'. Even when he gives up his throne to retire to a monastery, Constantine continues his regime of corruption and murder, coldly disposing of rivals and opponents. Several generations later we find Geraint, altogether a more sympathetic figure, referred to in AD705 by Adhelm, the first West Saxon bishop of Sherborne, as 'Geruntius, King of Dumnonia'. In fact, Geraint died heroically trying to protect his territory from the encroaching English kingdom of Wessex, struck down at the battle of Llongborth (perhaps present-day Langport in Somerset).

Later, in the **Annales Cambriae** (Welsh Annals) for the year AD875, we learn of the death by drowning of 'Dumnarth rex Cerniu' (Dumgarth, king of Cornwall), thought to be the 9th century Doniert whose memorial stone can to this day be found near St Cleer. Its Latin inscription reads DONIERT ROG-AVIT PRO ANIMA – 'Doniert has asked [prayers?] for [his] soul.' Presumably, Doniert was drowned in the swirling waters of nearby Golitha Falls on the River Fowey.

Left: The Doniert Stone
Right: Golitha Falls

# ATHELSTAN
# AND THE SAXONS

The last king of Cornwall, according to the **Anglo-Saxon Chronicle**, was 'Huwal [Hywel], king of the West Welsh' who was persuaded to recognise the overlordship of Athelstan, the ruthless and ambitious king of Wessex. Athelstan suceeded in welding the several Anglo-Saxon kingdoms together (to form the England we recognise today) as well as becoming the overlord of his Celtic neighbours. It was Athelstan who in AD936 fixed the River Tamar as the border between Cornwall and England, evicting the remaining Cornish from Exeter (and perhaps the rest of Devon) in an act in which, according to the later writer William of Malmesbury, that city was 'cleansed of its defilement by wiping out that filthy race'.

Dozmary Pool

Athelstan's settlement created the political and territorial Cornwall that still endures today, the culmination of a lengthy period of sporadic warfare in which the expansion of Anglo-Saxon Wessex had put increasing pressure on Dumnonia. The battle of Dyrham (Deorham) Down, near Bristol, in AD577 had driven an Anglo-Saxon wedge between the Celtic peoples of Wales and the South West peninsula. In AD682 it was reported that Centwine had driven the Celts as far as the sea (perhaps north-east Cornwall), and in AD710 Gereint was defeated by Ine, king of Wessex. In AD722 a combined Cornish and Danish force was defeated at 'Hehil', probably the strategically significant Camel estuary, and in AD838 a similar army of Cornish and Vikings was crushed at the great battle of Hingston Down, near Callington.

# KING ARTHUR

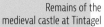
Remains of the
medieval castle at Tintagel

The story of Cornish resistance to the Anglo-Saxon advance is tied inextricably to the legend of King Arthur. Here again we have a tale of European high romance, taken to the continent by way of Celtic Brittany, whose origins seem rooted in Dark Age Cornwall. Of course, other parts of Britain, including Somerset, Wales, northern England and southern Scotland, also have their claims to Arthur, and perhaps we see in the King Arthur legend the collective exploits of not one but several heroic war-leaders who fought against the Anglo-Saxon intrusion in these islands.

At any rate, Cornwall has as good a claim as any to King Arthur. He appears in some versions of the Tristan and Iseult story, and sometimes too in the legend of Lyonnesse, the mythical lost land said to lie off the south-western tip of Cornwall. Associations with the Cornish landscape abound, especially in mid and North Cornwall. At Slaughter Bridge on the River Camel, for example, is the so-called 'Arthur's Grave', marked by an ancient inscribed stone (in reality a 5th or 6th century memorial to one Latinus), the supposed site, as Richard Carew wrote in 1602, of 'the last dismal battle' between King Arthur and his 'treacherous nephew Mordred'. Dozmary Pool, Castle-an-Dinas and Bossiney Mound all have Arthurian connections but the best known site of all is Tintagel Castle.

Tintagel's association with King Arthur was first proposed by Geoffrey of Monmouth in his 12th century **History of the Kings of Britain**. The castle ruins that we see today are clearly medieval but there is evidence of earlier occupation. Once thought to have been a Celtic monastery, the suggestion now is that the site was in Dark Age times a seat of Cornish royal power, a fortress so important that the Normans considered it politic to build a castle there, with Geoffrey of Monmouth wedding it firmly to the Arthur legend. Here Geoffrey and his Norman patrons were playing to the Cornish gallery, for medieval Cornish (and Breton) people believed that Arthur was not dead but would come again to be their king. The Canons of Laon were told this when they visited Cornwall in 1113, and there was great offence when they suggested that the story might not be true.

# THE LAND OF
# THE SAINTS

If Cornwall is the land of Arthur, then it is also most assuredly the land of saints. An old adage insists that 'there are more saints in Cornwall than in Heaven', and many enthusiasts today see Cornwall as the hub of a Dark Age 'Celtic Christianity' whose spokes reached out to Brittany, Ireland, Wales, Scotland, the Isle of Man and even Galicia in northern Spain, accounting for the multiplicity of Cornish church dedications to Celtic Saints such as Piran, Petroc, Goran, Columb and Winwaloe.

In fact, Christianity probably did not arrive in Cornwall until the 6th century, and when it did come it was as a result of the settlement here of nobles of Irish descent from the kingdom of Demetia (in what is today south-west Wales). These settlers are recorded in the numerous inscribed memorial stones of the period, the earliest inscribed in Ogham (the mysterious Irish stroke alphabet), later ones in both Ogham and Latin, and those later still in Latin only.

These stones help us to chart the conversion of Cornwall to Christianity, and emphasise the importance of Latin to the spread of Christian teaching. Good examples of bi-lingual stones are those at St Kew (inscribed in Latin as IVSTI – 'of Justus' – a name repeated in Ogham) and Lewannick. At Lewannick there are two stones, one within the church which commemorates a certain Ulcagnus, and another in the churchyard in memory of one Igenavus.

Other early indications of Christian influence are the chi-ro monograms inscribed on slabs, such as those at Phillack, St Erth, South Hill and St Endellion. The extent to which Welsh or Irish dedications in Cornwall actually represent the missionary activities of 'saints' from those areas is open to dispute, and it may be, for example, that the many of the Welsh church dedications – St Breock, St Teath, St Mabyn, St Issey, and so on – reflect the influence of Wales rather than the actual presence of Welsh holy men and women. However, in the 7th century Vita Sancti Samsonis, the Life of St Samson of Dol in Brittany, we do have a fascinating insight into the work of one Welsh monastic missionary who was active in Cornwall in the early days of Cornish Christianity. Samson arrived from Wales on the shores of the Camel estuary, making his way down the Camel-Fowey route (today popularised as 'The Saints' Way') to travel across to Brittany. During his sojourn in Cornwall he converted many people from their pagan ways, on one occasion disposing of a fearful serpent that had lurked in a cave near Fowey.

Other, more fanciful, stories of saints' exploits also survive – such as those that tell us that St Piran (a Patron of Cornwall, along with St Petroc and St Michael) floated across from Ireland on a millstone, or that St Ia arrived on a giant leaf.

St Mawes Castle

Samson's journey to Brittany reminds us that the links between the Cornish and Bretons were already close. In time, many Cornish church dedications would echo those of Brittany. St Mewan, whose parish in Cornwall adjoins that of St Austell, is also remembered at St Méen in eastern Brittany. St Mawes (near Falmouth) is commemorated in Brittany at Ile Maudez and Lamodez, while St Winwaloe – patron of Gunwalloe and Landewednack on the Lizard, of Tremaine in North Cornwall, and of St Winnolls near Torpoint – is in his Breton guise St Gwénolé, founder of the great monastery of Landévennec. However, the links between Cornwall and Brittany pre-dated this Christian 'Age of Saints', and perhaps as early as AD300 there was widespread settlement of immigrants from south-west Britain in Brittany.

Suggestions that these immigrants may have been fleeing the pressure of Irish colonisation in Cornwall or the first signs of Anglo-Saxon intrusion have been supplemented recently by new arguments that there may have been an official settlement policy in operation, designed to colonise sparsely populated areas. But whatever the explanation, these immigrants seem to have been in full control of the Breton peninsula by AD500, accounting amongst other things for the close similarity of the Cornish and Breton languages.

The presence of the prefix 'Lan' (meaning a holy enclosure, comparable to Welsh Llan) in Cornish and Breton placenames such as Landewednack (Cornwall) and Landévennec (Brittany) helps us to identify early monastic sites.

By the 9th century 'Lannaled' (St Germans) had become the pre-eminent monastery in Cornwall, and by the 10th century the monastery of St Petroc at Bodmin was also prominent. The Domesday Book listed a number of Cornish religious houses: St Germans, St Petroc, St Piran, St Carantoc, St Achebran (St Keverne), St Buryan and St Neot. Others were at St Michael's Mount, St Goran, Constantine, Lammana (Looe Island), and St Anthony-in-Roseland.

By now Celtic crosses were appearing across Cornwall (St Piran's, at Perranzabuloe, is dated to before AD960), evidence perhaps of a distinctively 'Celtic' style of religious iconography, although in AD1046 the briefly independent Cornish diocese was reincorporated into that of Crediton, an indication that – a hundred years or so after Athelstan's settlement – Cornwall's residual semi-independence was conditional upon the will of Anglo-Saxon England.

Celtic Cross

# THE EARLDOM AND DUCHY OF CORNWALL

A view of Launceston in 1829. Whilst the height of the Castle is slightly exaggerated, it was always intended to overawe the town and the neighbouring countryside. Launceston was the Assize town.

The Norman Conquest in 1066 brought changing conditions, not least a renewed impetus to the relationship between Cornwall and Brittany and to the cult of King Arthur. There had been many Bretons in William's army at the Battle of Hastings, and the Normans in Cornwall secured the legitimacy of their rule by deploying both the Breton connection and the Arthurian myth. The Cornish language, already under pressure from the spread of English, may even have enjoyed a period of resurgence under Norman and Breton patronage.

An Earldom of Cornwall was established, and when about 1173 Earl Reginald granted freedoms and privileges to the burgesses of Truro, he was careful to address them to 'the barons of Cornwall, and all men both Cornish and English'.

In 1337 the Earldom was reinvented by Edward III as the Duchy of Cornwall. He proclaimed his son, the seven-year old Black Prince, Duke of Cornwall and decided that henceforth the Duchy lands should always be the source of revenue for the Heir Apparent who, in turn, would always be Duke. Edward III was mindful that he was building this Duchy upon not only the Earldom but also an earlier line of indigenous Cornish rulers, advancing 'our most dear first begotten Edward...to be Duke of Cornwall, over which awhile ago Dukes for a long time successively presided as chief rulers'. Moreover, he was clear that Cornwall was one of 'the remarkable places in our kingdoms', a view echoed very much later by the Duchy of Cornwall itself in 1855-57 in its own historical survey of the Duchy Charters of 1337 and 1338. This survey concluded that 'the Duke was quasi-sovereign within his Duchy' and that 'Cornwall was distinct from England, and under separate government... Cornwall, like Wales, was at the time of the Conquest, and was subsequently treated in many respects as, distinct from England'.

To this constitutional semi-independence was added the signi-ficant influence of the Duchy over medieval Cornish society and economy, much of which served to emphasise

13

Cornwall's 'difference', particularly in the large tracts of land that were actually owned by the Duchy. For example, there were few 'manors' in Cornwall in the English sense, and on Duchy manors there was little evidence of the open-field, strip system of agriculture so typical of the English manorial system.

That is not to say that there were not examples of strip farming elsewhere in Cornwall (notably around the larger settlements such as Penryn and Helston) but even at this date the high stone and earth hedges, small fields and winding lanes that are typical of Cornwall today were already characteristic of those areas enclosed for agriculture.

The distinctive qualities of the Duchy's influence were also evident in the 'free' tenancies in operation on Duchy lands, with seven-year leases at market prices and only negligible services required in return, a marked contrast to the 'bonded' or 'serf' labour encountered in feudal England and a precursor, perhaps, of the independent and potentially mobile small farmers who came to characterise Cornwall. Similarly, the influence of the Duchy served to inhibit the emergence of a powerful (and potentially rival) gentry. There were few great independent landowners, and in 1602 Richard Carew could note wryly in his **Survey of Cornwall** that 'so for noblemen I may deliver a word, that Cornwall at this present enjoyeth the residence of none at all'. Moreover, 'most Cornish gentlemen can better vaunt of their pedigree than their livelihood'.

The Duchy also encouraged the diversification of the medieval Cornish economy, and between the twelfth and fourteenth centuries there was economic and population growth. When the Black Death struck in 1349 and again in 1360 some areas of settlement, notably on the moors, were abandoned but the relative strength of the Cornish economy protected Cornwall from the worst effects of the plague. Indeed, the Hundred Years War with France proved a further stimulus to economic activity, particularly for the southern ports of Saltash, Looe and Fowey. There were Cornish ships in the great fleet that defeated the French at Sluys in 1340, and by the middle of the 14th century, as the conflict drew to a close, Landulph, Saltash, Fowey, Mevagissey, Truro, Penryn, Marazion and Penzance were all supplying transport vessels for the war effort.

In addition to this maritime activity, other towns such as Mitchell and Wadebridge grew up along the spinal trading and communication routes, while others such as Tregony and Week St Mary served as centres for their rural hinterlands. The Duchy, like the Earldom before it, also encouraged the establishment of towns and boroughs, such as Camelford, Bodmin, Launceston, Liskeard and Lostwithiel.

However, despite the economic diversification that such expansion implied, by the late medieval period tin mining was emerging as a central feature of the Cornish economy. By the end of the 14th century, the focus of this industry was moving from East Cornwall (where moorland tin-streaming predominated) to the more westerly districts where streaming was also practised but where new open-cut and (increasingly) underground mining was developed.

The importance of the tin industry was mirrored in the prestige and influence of the Stannaries, an institution (or series of institutions) that had grown up in the early medieval period to establish the rights, privileges and governance of the Cornish tinners. Although sharing much in common with other 'free mining' areas such as the Forest of Dean, the Mendips and even neighbouring Dartmoor, the Stannary system as it developed in Cornwall went much further to provide what were in effect the legal and political institutions of semi-independence. A Charter of 1201 established the four mining districts – or 'Stannaries' – in which Stannary Law might operate: Foweymore (modern Bodmin Moor), Blackmore (today the china clay country around St Austell), Tywarnhaile (the area around Truro and St Agnes), and Penwith-with-Kerrier in the west. There was also a Stannary Parliament, both representing and making laws for these Stannaries. When the Duchy of Cornwall was created in 1337, the Stannaries were brought within its orbit, marshalling its institutions to those of the Duchy (the Lord Warden of the Stannaries became one of the most important Duchy offices) and controlling tin 'coinage', the tax payable on smelted tin which became an important part of Duchy income.

Although the writ of Stannary law was confined theoretically to the four mining districts, there was no attempt to define where the boundaries of these Stannaries might be; as the whole of Cornwall was potentially metalliferous, it was sometimes argued that the jurisdiction of the Stannary Parliament and Courts could be interpreted as running (as the Duchy did) to all parts of the territory of Cornwall. As the Duchy itself argued in its survey of 1855-57, the Stannaries, Duchy and County of Cornwall were seen as territorially co-terminous: 'the Stannary unquestionably extended over the whole County, it is manifest that the term Duchy was used in an equally extensive sense'. It is no surprise that medieval official documents sometimes referred to **Anglia et Cornubia**, England and Cornwall, much like today's phrase 'England-and-Wales'.

# THE CORNISH LANGUAGE

Indeed, in addition to the constitutional (and socio-economic) distinctiveness described above, Cornwall's enduring separate identity was in the medieval period reflected in the Cornish language and its literature, and in continuing links with Brittany. Although under pressure from the encroaching English language even before the Norman Conquest, Cornish proved remarkably resilient for much of the period. It may have benefited, as noted above, from Norman and Breton patronage after 1066, and some scholars have argued that the area in which the language was spoken actually increased in subsequent centuries, so that even in 1500 it may in some places have been spoken right up to the River Tamar. However, most agree that there was a process of gradual retreat during this period, so that by 1500 the language had fallen back to the Fowey-Camel line in mid-Cornwall.

Nonetheless, this meant that Cornish was still spoken in just over half the territory of Cornwall by about half the total population, estimated at 69,000. Moreover, Cornish would have been familiar to many other people in Cornwall as a result of trading contacts or pilgrimage, even if not understood. It would certainly still have been heard on the quaysides and in the taverns of such places as East and West Looe or at Bodmin on market day. In 1542 Andrew Boorde summed up the state of the Cornish language: 'In Cornwall is two speches; the one is naughty Englyshe, and the other Cornyshe speche. And there may be many men and women the which cannot speake one word of Englyshe, but all Cornyshe'.

As one might expect, it is through the activities of the Church in medieval Cornwall that we gain insights into the state of the Cornish language. A single sentence dating from 1265 in what is known as 'Old Cornish', the earliest form of the language, refers to the founding of the church of St Thomas at Glasney, Penryn, and to the story in which St Thomas was said to have appeared in a dream to the Bishop of Exeter, commanding him to establish a church at Polsethow in Penryn. The punning sentence tells us: **'In Polsethow ywhylyr anethow,'** in which **'anethow'** has two meanings, 'dwellings' and 'marvels', giving us the deliberately ambiguous translation 'In Polsethow shall be seen dwellings [or marvels].'

When Bishop John de Grandisson preached at St Buryan, in the far west of Cornwall, in 1328 or 1329 his sermon had to be translated into Cornish for the benefit of his monoglot congregation. In 1339 he appointed J Polmarke to preach in the Cornish language at St Merryn, near Padstow, and in 1354-55 he appointed two penitentiaries in Cornwall – one in Truro for those who spoke only Cornish and one in Bodmin for those who spoke Cornish and English.

Later, in 1538, it was decreed that the Epistle or Gospel of the Day might be read in Cornish in those parishes where English was not understood, and even as late as 1560 it was directed by the Bishop that those who spoke no English could be taught the Catechism in Cornish.

*Stained glass at St Neot* ©Andrew Besley

Such concessions reflected the tenacity of the Cornish language, even in mid-Cornwall. As late as 1587 an interpreter had to be provided for certain fishermen from Gorran Haven (near Mevagissey in mid-Cornwall) who knew no English, while the neighbouring parish of St Ewe had bilingual inhabitants in 1595.

However, the Church in medieval Cornwall seems also to have been genuinely sympathetic to Cornish, not least at the collegiate church of Glasney, Penryn, which emerged as a major centre of ecclesiastical scholarship in the language, conferring upon it status and worth. There is an extensive literature in medieval Cornish, or 'Middle Cornish' as it is known, and much of this appears to have been written at Glasney. The **Ordinalia**, for example, is thought to have been composed at Glasney, a miracle play consisting of three separate components which together took a full three days to perform, the venue being an open-air plen-an-gwarry or 'playing place'. A religious cycle, the **Ordinalia** commences with the creation of the world, and charts the experience of Adam from his 'fall' in the Garden of Eden to his eventual restoration to Heaven through the redeeming sacrifice of Jesus Christ.

A later play, **Gwreans an Bys** (the Creation of the World), echoes in part the themes and content of the **Ordinalia**. Although the manu-script that has survived is a 1611 copy made by William Jordan of Helston, **Gwreans an Bys** is thought to date originally from about 1530-40. Again, the purpose is strictly religious, detailing the struggle between Good and Evil and recording the eventual triumph of the former:

| | |
|---|---|
| *Gallas Lucifer, droke preve,* | Gone is Lucifer the snake, |
| *Mes an Nef tha dewolgowe* | out of heaven to dark hell. |
| *Ha lemyn un y lea ef* | Now, without fail I shall make, |
| *Me a vyn heb falladowe,* | to take and fill his place well, |
| *Un dean formya* | a new-formed man |
| *In valy Ebron devery.* | in the Valley of Hebron. |
| *Rag collenwall aredy* | And the man shall fill, anon, |
| *An le may teth anotha.* | the place from which he was banned. |

The importance of the Church in medieval Cornish life is reflected in the scores of Celtic crosses still to be found across Cornwall, together with holy wells such as those of Sancreed and Madron, St Cleer and Dupath, St Keyne and St Clether. Nicholas Roscarrock, the Cornish Catholic and hagiographer, recorded in the 17th century how on St Piran's Day (5th March) the saint's relics were carried from one parish to the next in an act of pilgrimage and veneration, while local Celtic saints continued to be revered throughout the medieval period.

Where parishes did not have Celtic dedications, the locals were not above inventing them – such as St Morvetha at Morvah in 1390 or St Tallandus at Talland in 1452. This enthusiasm was also reflected in the rebuilding of many Cornish churches in the 15th century, when most acquired their distinctive three-stage Cornish towers, and when (in the early 16th century) the glorious stained glass windows that still survive were installed in St Neot.

Intriguingly, Breton craftsmen seemed to have had a particular part to play in this late medieval refurbishment of Cornish churches, hinting at the intimate relations that still existed between Cornwall and Brittany. For example, Breton carpenters were in 1523-24 paid £58 for completion of the timber rood-loft at North Petherwin, while at Bodmin in 1529-30 others were hired to set up seats and dismantle the organ. The well-house at Dupath and the spire of Lostwithiel church may also betray Breton influence.

Certainly, as well as the routine passage of pilgrims, traders and sailors between Cornwall and Brittany, there were many Breton settlers in Cornwall during this period – in western, Cornish-speaking parishes such as St Ives, Towednack, Zennor, Lelant and Constantine but also in the east in maritime areas like Fowey, Polruan and East Looe.

As we have seen already, the Duchy and the Stannaries together served to create an aura (and indeed reality) of Cornish semi-independence, reinforcing the cultural 'difference' embodied in the Cornish language and the links with Brittany, but at the same time wedding Cornwall tightly to the interests and needs of the Crown, establishing in effect the political relationship between 'periphery' and 'centre'. When, in the late medieval era, the power of the 'centre' waned, so the 'periphery' (Ireland, Wales and Scotland as well as Cornwall) was left very much to its own devices, precipitating in Cornwall what the late AL Rowse called a mood of 'feudal anarchy'. During the Wars of the Roses in the 15th century the influence of the Duchy declined, reflecting the dislocation caused by civil conflict. Increasing lawlessness (much of it politically motivated by rival Lancastrian and Yorkist sympathisers) became apparent in Cornwall. Henry Bodrugan, a member of the lesser gentry and Cornwall's leading Yorkist, was notorious even in his own time for acts of violence, burglary and piracy. He was rewarded by Richard III for his efforts but in 1485 when Henry Tudor won the Crown at the Battle of Bosworth Field, all this was undone.

Zennor Church

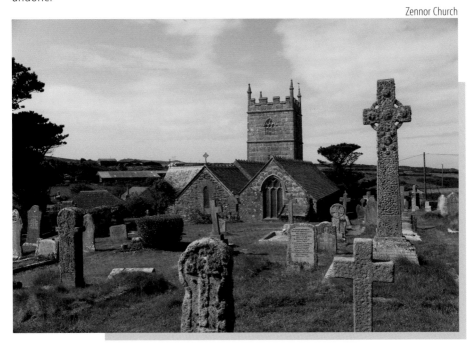

# HENRY TUDOR

In fact, most Cornish people had supported the cause of Henry Tudor, siding with the Lancastrians and becoming embroiled in a resurrection of the Arthurian myth: this was in effect the first act of a 'British project' which in the modern period created the United Kingdom. Henry Tudor claimed not only the throne of England but asserted his right to a 'Greater Britain', protesting his Welshness and insisting on his direct descent from Arthur himself. His exile in Brittany had further enhanced his Celtic credentials (he was proclaimed Henry VII at Bodmin even before he had returned to fight at Bosworth Field), and when he did fight Richard III for the Crown he flew the Welsh dragon as his standard, with Welshmen and Cornishmen at his side. His first-born son, the Duke of Cornwall, he called Arthur (though the boy did not live long), and in giving preferment to his Welsh and Cornish supporters, he sent Richard Edgcumbe (who had already driven Henry Bodrugan from Cornwall) on diplomatic missions to Ireland, Scotland and Brittany to try to establish his new order.

However, inherent in Henry Tudor's project was the need for the 'centre' to re-establish its control of the 'periphery', to tackle the 'feudal anarchy' (or rather, the decline in English influence) that had come to characterise Cornwall and other parts of these islands by introducing what has become known to modern historians as 'the Tudor revolution in government'. This was a lengthy process, with fits and starts and points of near collapse. It was continued by Henry VIII and under the boy-king Edward VI, and busied itself with a range of measures, from price controls and a new state-wide system of poor relief to the re-organisation of the administration of Wales (the Act of Union in 1536) and the subjugation of the hitherto rebellious North of England. Significant elements of this project were the introduction of more systematic taxation and, later, of the Reformation. Both of these were to have a traumatic impact upon Cornwall.

In 1495-96 the Council of Prince Arthur, Duke of Cornwall, announced new rules for the regulation of the tin mining industry. The Cornish tinners, so used to their independence, reacted angrily to this intervention, creating an ugly mood in Cornwall which was made worse in 1497 when new taxes were raised to pay for a war against the Scots. As the 17th century chronicler, Francis Bacon, put it: 'For no sooner began the subsidy [tax] to be levied in Cornwall, but the people there began to grudge and murmur'. And as Bacon added warily, the Cornish were a formidable people: 'The Cornish being a race of men stout of stomach, mighty of body and limb, and that lived hardly in a barren country, and many of them could for a need live under ground that were tinners'.

Meanwhile, Henry VII was incensed that the Cornish had largely ignored the new rules introduced by Prince Arthur's Council and angrily confiscated the Stannary Charters, in effect suspending Stannary government in Cornwall. Taken together, the suspension of the Stannaries and the imposition of a tax for a purpose that the Cornish argued had nothing to do with them made Cornwall ripe for rebellion.

A memorial to Michael Joseph and Thomas Flamank at St Keverne

The first signs of uprising were in the remote parish of St Keverne, on the Lizard peninsula, where Michael Joseph An Gof, 'the Smith', the local blacksmith, emerged as a popular and outspoken leader. At Bodmin Thomas Flamank, a lawyer, argued the legal case against the new tax. People flocked to the rebel cause from all over Cornwall, not only the ordinary folk but yeomen and lesser gentry too, men such as John Rosewarne of Rosewarne (near Camborne), John Trevysall of Madron, Richard Borlase of St Wenn and John Allen of Stoke Climsland. The contemporary historian, Polydore Vergil, writing in his Anglica Historia, observed that 'While the people were thus in ferment, two men out of the scum of the people, namely Thomas Flammock [sic], a lawyer, and Michael Joseph, a blacksmith, two bold rascals, put themselves at the head of the rising'. As Vergil added, 'When they saw that the mob was aroused they kept shouting that it was a scandalous crime that the king, in order to make a small expedition against the Scots, should burden the wretched men of Cornwall, who either cultivated a barren soil, or with difficulty sought a living by digging tin.'

Wheal Coates

Despite their fury, the Cornish rebels caused little or no damage as they marched to London, gathering supporters on their way and fighting a brief skirmish at Guildford before arriving at Blackheath. There, overlooking Greenwich Palace, they threatened the English political establishment at its very heart, posing for Henry VII the greatest crisis of his reign. However, the 15,000 or so Cornish were confronted by the huge professional army, some 25,000 strong, that had been marshalled for the war against Scotland. It was this might that was turned against the men of Cornwall on Blackheath battlefield. Although many rebels had stolen away during the night, the Cornish put up a brave fight, especially in its opening phases. Cornish archers had won a formidable reputation in earlier days against the French at Crécy and Agincourt, and at Blackheath they were said to have 'wrought wonders', Bacon noting that 'On the King's part there died, about 300, most of them shot with arrows, which were reported to be the length of a tailor's yard, so strong and mighty a bow the Cornishmen were said to draw.' In fact, there is some doubt as to the extent of the casualties, estimates of Cornish losses, for example, ranging from 200 to 2000. However, superior numbers won the day. Thomas Flamank and Michael Joseph were both captured and on 27 June 1497 were drawn on a hurdle from the Tower of London to Tyburn where they were hanged, drawn and quartered, Michael Joseph shouting defiantly that he 'should have a name perpetual, and a fame permanent and immortal'.

In the aftermath of the battle, Henry VII proved remarkably sparing of blood, perhaps out of genuine compassion or maybe remembering his 'Arthuran' credentials, preferring fines to execution in his pacification of Cornwall. However, Cornish feelings still ran high and when Perkin Warbeck, a pretender to the throne, arrived in Cornwall in September 1497, some 6000 rebels were prepared to join him for a new march on London. This time, however, they got no further than Taunton, where Warbeck lost his nerve and deserted his supporters. Again, Henry VII was remarkably sparing of blood but his fines were a heavy burden on Cornwall. Some Cornish gentlemen were outlawed, their lands confiscated. That the Cornish remained angry is suggested in one of the miracle plays, written at about this time (probably at Glasney) entitled Beunans Meriasek (the 'Life of St Meriasek') and performed in 1504. Composed in the Cornish language, which the English could not understand, the play in places has a subversive feel, especially those scenes dealing with the evil King Teudar (a thinly-veiled reference to Henry Tudor, perhaps) and his opponent, the good Duke of Cornwall.

Teudar, although an outsider, insists that, 'Teudar me a veth gelwys, arluth regnijs in kernow/Teudar I am called, Lord reigning in Cornwall'. He later threatens that:

| | |
|---|---|
| *Duk Kernow hag oll y dus,* | Duke of Cornwall and all his folk, |
| *Indan ov threys me as glus* | Under my feet I will crush them |
| *Poren kepar ha treysy.* | Just like grains of sand. |

It appears that Henry VII recognised that the Cornish were not yet pacified, and decided that he should resort to new measures to win back the loyalty of Cornwall. By 1500 many of those outlawed were already pardoned and being given back their land, while in 1508 Henry VII proclaimed his 'Charter of Pardon' which restored Stannary governance, this time with new powers, including the right of the Stannary Parliament to overturn any law made at Westminster.

# THE LATER TUDORS

When Henry VIII became king in 1509, it was noted by one observer that each of the great horses that led his Coronation procession was bedecked in the coat of arms of one or other of his presumed possessions: 'as of England and France, Gascony, Guienne, Normandy, Anjou, Cornwall, Wales, Ireland, wrought upon velvets with embroidery and goldsmith's worth'.

Henry VIII also promised to create a new Cornish diocese, although he spent the money earmarked for the project on his wars with France, but he is especially remembered for his contribution to the 'Tudor revolution in government' – the Reformation. The break with Catholic Rome and the creation of the Church of England caused widespread upheaval, not least in Cornwall where the new religious ways were resisted vigorously. Henry VIII died in 1547 but his work was continued under his son, the boy-king Edward VI. In April 1548 William Body, who had purchased a lease on the archdeaconry of Cornwall, arrived in Helston to remove 'popish' images from the parish church. However, he was confronted by an angry mob, led by Martin Geoffrey, priest of St Keverne, and William and John Kilter, yeomen of Constantine, and soon killed. There were reprisals, with some of the ringleaders executed, and Cornwall was again sliding towards rebellion.

In January 1549 the Act of Uniformity was passed, one of whose provisions was a new Book of Common Prayer. Imposed from outside and in a language (English) that many Cornish could not understand, this new prayer book was met with almost universal hostility in Cornwall. At Bodmin, insurgents rallied around the mayor, Henry Bray, and two local leaders of the Catholic gentry, Humphry Arundell of Helland (whose grandfather had risen in 1497) and John Winslade of Tregarrick. Support for this new rebel cause came from all across Cornwall, from the monoglot Cornish-speaking west but also from other parts, from individuals such as Thomas Holmes of Blisland, Robert Smith of St Germans, and Simon Morton, vicar of Poundstock.

A petition was drawn up, declaring that the new Service was 'like a Christmas game... we will have our old service of Mattins, Mass, Evensong and procession in Latin as it was before'. Significantly, the rebels added: 'And we the Cornish men (whereof certain of us understand no English) utterly refuse this new English.' Archbishop Cranmer retorted that there were more in Cornwall who knew English than Latin but he was missing the point, for Latin was familiar across Cornwall (if not always understood) while English was not.

River Tamar

Soon the rebels moved out of Cornwall, crossing the Tamar to join the people of Sampford Courtenay near Okehampton, who had also risen against the prayer book, the Dartmoor tinners in this period often having more in common with their Cornish colleagues than with folk elsewhere in Devon. Together, they laid siege to Exeter, the Cornish archers again performing to good effect, although they were persuaded by the vicar of St Thomas, Father Welsh, a Cornishman, not to shoot fire-balls into the city, thereby saving it from destruction. Meanwhile, an army under Lord Russell was already heading west to confront the rebels, and battle was joined at Fenny Bridges, to the east of Exeter. As John Hooker, the Devon historian who himself experienced the siege, recorded, 'The fight for the time was very sharp and cruel, for the Cornishmen were very lusty and fresh and fully bent to fight out the matter'.

The rebels were pushed back but Russell dared not pursue them until further reinforcements arrived under Lord Grey. Fearing attack, Russell ordered that all prisoners be slaughtered, and on 5 August 1549, his army swollen by reinforcements, he engaged the Cornish at Clyst Honiton. Lord Grey found himself embroiled in a battle that he later reflected was harder fought than any he had known in any war but, as in 1497, superior numbers and weaponry carried the day. The rebels were scattered, although a stiff rearguard action was fought at Sampford Courtenay as the rebels retreated to the Tamar.

In contrast to 1497, the aftermath of the 1549 rebellion was cruel and ruthless. Some thousands had died on the battlefield, and what followed was equally bloody. Father Welsh, the Cornishman who had saved Exeter, was hanged from his church tower and in Cornwall priests implicated in the rising were singled out for particular attention. Simon Morton, priest of Poundstock, was executed, as was Richard Bennett, the vicar of St Veep and St Neot, together with those of Gulval and Pillaton. Amongst those outlawed were the vicars of St Cleer, St Keverne, and Uny Lelant. The pacification of Cornwall was left to one Sir Anthony Kingston. In Bodmin he asked the new mayor, Nicholas Boyer, to prepare a scaffold upon which to execute captured rebels. When Boyer showed Kingston his work, Kingston asked the mayor whether the gallows were strong enough. Boyer replied that they were, at which point Kingston quipped 'Well then get you even up to them, for they are provided for you... You have been a busy rebel, and therefore this is your appointed reward'. It is said that Kingston played the same trick with equal success when dealing with John Payne, the portreeve of St Ives, and other grim stories are told of the grisly pleasure Kingston took in his subjugation of Cornwall.

One of the chief casualties of 1549 was the Cornish language. The death of so many Cornish people was itself a blow to the community of language speakers, while the closure of Glasney College as part of the Dissolution of the Monasteries deprived Cornish of a centre of learning as well as status.

Moreover, the prayer book and Bible were never translated into Cornish, as they were into Welsh; the language was perhaps now irrevocably tainted as a 'popish' or rebel tongue and unlikely to win many advocates. John Norden, writing soon after in the reign of Elizabeth, reported that 'of late the Cornish men have much conformed themselves to the use of the English tongue', adding that 'it seems that in a few years the Cornish language will be by little and little abandoned'. Something of a respite had been provided by the short reign of Mary Tudor (1553-58), when Catholicism had become briefly once again the official religion and when Bishop Edmund Bonner's homilies were translated into Cornish by one John Tregear (the so-called Tregear Homilies), but essentially Norden was correct in his analysis, though the language was to prove more tenacious among the common people than he had supposed.

Roman Catholicism retained stubborn support in some parts of Cornwall and amongst some Cornish families, notably the Arundells of Lanherne and the Tregians of Golden near Probus. It found a literary voice in the work of the 17th century hagiographer Nicholas Roscarrock, author of the Lives of the Saints, who was sent to the Tower for his pains.

Yet increasingly Cornish people came to conform to the Protestant religion. This was especially so as relations with Spain deteriorated, when Cornwall was suddenly in the front line and of enormous strategic importance to England. The Cornish gentry were wooed with the granting of numerous town charters, leading in time to the situation where Cornwall sent no fewer than 44 MPs to Westminster. Cornish privateers and pirates – such as the notorious Killigrew family of Arwenack, Falmouth – made money out of the confrontations with Spain. Richard Grenville of Stowe came to epitomise the new generation of Cornish sea-dogs who championed the cause of Protestantism against the threat of Catholic Spain, in 1591 dying heroically in his ship the Revenge as it battled single-handedly against 53 Spanish vessels. New castles had been built in 1540 at Pendennis and St Mawes to resist any Spanish invasion but the Spanish Armada of 1588 passed Cornwall by. When the Spaniards did choose to attack Cornwall, on 23 July 1595, they selected Mount's Bay and landed a raiding party of some 200 men to sack Mousehole and burn Paul church. Off the coast of Mousehole is Merlin's Rock and so, it was said, was fulfilled the ancient Cornish prophecy:

*Ewra teyre a war mearne Merlyn*
*Ara lesky Pawle Pensanz ha Newlyn.*

They shall land on the Rock of Merlin
Who shall burn Paul, Penzance and Newlyn.

# RICHARD CAREW'S
# SURVEY OF CORNWALL

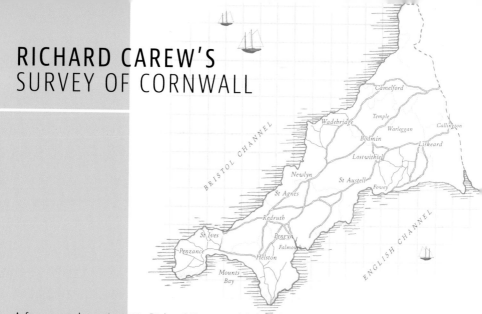

A few years later, in 1602, Richard Carew published his Survey of Cornwall, a book that tells us much about Cornwall at the time but also about Carew himself and the other Cornish gentry. We see in his Survey a genuine pride in Cornwall, for example in its archers and its wrestlers and hurlers, as well as real affection for the Cornish people, particularly the gentry, remarking that they are all 'cousins' and providing charming pen-pictures of folk such as 'Mr Thomas Peyton [of Ardevora], a gentleman for his age and virtue deserving a regardful estimation' and 'Master Glyn of Glynfoord [who] manifesteth, by this compounded name, the antiquity of his descent'.

But Carew is also a Renaissance man, championing the superiority of the English language above all others, describing it as 'our natural language' and asserting its 'excellency', at the same time demonstrating his limited and inaccurate knowledge of Cornish in offering such translations as 'The Miry Head' for 'Pulstean' (it means tin pool or pit). And, although he concedes that the English spoken by the common Cornish is 'good and pure', having learned it 'from the best hands of their own gentry and the eastern merchants', he is embarrassed that 'they disgrace it in part with a broad and rude accent'. He offers coded apologies for the 'commotions' of 1497 and 1549 and, in a further demonstration of his cultural distance from his countrymen, his description of what must have been the dying days of the 'gwary miracle' (Carew's phrase) hints at a restrained contempt for the harmless fun gleaned by ordinary folk from what had become chaotic parodies. Actors deliberately fluffed their lines but it did not matter, he said, for 'it defrauded not the beholders, but dismissed them with a great deal more sport and laughter than twenty such gwaries could have afforded'.

# THE
# CIVIL WAR

It is significant that Carew came from Antony, in the south-eastern tip of Cornwall, an area in which similar Renaissance views to his own gained currency with the local gentry during the 17th century, not least in adherence to Puritanism, the Calvinistic strand of Protestantism that was (amongst other things) to motivate the Parliamentarian side during the Civil Wars of the period. Elsewhere in south-east Cornwall, gentry such as the Robartes of Lanhydrock and the Eliots of St Germans espoused Puritan and Parliamentarian sentiments as the crisis of Charles I's reign developed, although, as elsewhere in Cornwall, the common people held to a conservative Royalism that resented assaults on their beliefs from outside. But when, during 1642, it became clear that the conflict between King and Parliament might lead to war, many of the Cornish gentry (though not the more determined Puritans, such as the Robartes family) put their religious and political differences to one side to declare loyalty to the Crown.

Intriguingly, in the conduct of the Civil War in Cornwall, and in the motivations of the Cornish as well as in the attitudes to Cornwall displayed by outsiders, we hear more than an echo of the passions and events of 1497 and 1549. The minority of Parliamentarian sympathisers took refuge in Puritan Plymouth, while Sir Beville Grenville of Stowe emerged as the focus of the Royalist cause in Cornwall.

Almost immediately, Cornwall acquired its reputation as a bulwark of Royalism. When a Parliamentarian army ventured into Cornwall in January 1643 it was soundly beaten by the Cornish army at Braddock Down, near Liskeard, while a second Roundhead incursion that April suffered a similar fate at Stamford Hill, near Stratton. The Royalist journal Mercurius Aulicus drew a telling comparison between Cornwall and similarly Royalist Wales, noting that only Pembrokeshire, so-called Little England beyond Wales, 'forsook their allegiance when all other Welch counties stood loyal to his Majestie; so Cornwall (which is little Wales beyond England) proved themselves true Brittaines when no English county stood entirely for his Majestie.' But if the Royalists approved of the Cornish, the Roundheads categorised them along with the Welsh and Irish as 'pagans' and 'heathens', one complaining of 'Hellish Cornwall'; another insisting that 'the men of Cornwall are very hea-thens, a corner of ignorants, and atheists, drained from the mines'.

Pendennis Castle, Falmouth

Taking the offensive, the Cornish army now crossed the Tamar, defeating the Parliamentarians at the battles of Lansdowne (near Bath) and Roundway Down (but with the terrible loss of Sir Beville Grenville at the former) and going on to participate in the captures of Bristol and Lyme Regis. Attempting to reverse their fortunes in Cornwall, a Parliamentarian force under Lord Essex crossed the Tamar in July 1644, penetrating as far as Bodmin and torching the Duchy Palace (a symbol of both Cornish Royalism and Cornish independence) at Lostwithiel. But the Roundheads were in hostile country: Essex noted that 'the country people are more bloody than the enemy', and his army was soundly defeated at Fowey and Lostwithiel. Indeed, of the 7000 Parliamentarian soldiers who marched into the 'Cornish mousetrap', as it was known, only 1000 escaped back across the Tamar. Hot on the heels of this humiliating defeat, newly raised Cornish recruits laid siege to Plymouth, though it proved too difficult a nut to crack, but elsewhere the war was not going well for the Royalists.

The Prince of Wales, Duke of Cornwall, later to become Charles II, took refuge in Cornwall, his trusted Duchy. But Sir Richard Grenville, the late Beville's brother, urged the Duke to make a separate peace with the Parliamentarians, to establish Cornwall as a semi-independent Royalist statelet. Prince Charles was determined to fight on but he was soon obliged to flee into exile on the Continent, while the Royalist army surrendered formally at Tresillian Bridge on 12 March 1646. St Michael's Mount held out for another month, and Pendennis clung on until the August when finally John Arundell – 'Jack for the King' – marched out of the castle with 'colours flying, trumpets sounding, drums beating'. The Civil War was over in Cornwall, save for a spirited but doomed insurrection in May 1648 which ended in the 'Gear rout' near Helston, and the resistance of the Scilly garrison until 1651.

Although there were calls for the reduction of Cornwall as punishment for the fate of Essex's army, the Parliamentarian treatment of Cornwall was remarkably restrained. Some gentry lost their lands, some priests were driven from their livings, notably the vicars of Ludgvan, Lanivet, St Cleer, St Goran, St Keverne, St Buryan, and Warbstow, and the Duchy of Cornwall was abolished. Cornwall's parliamentary representation was cut to twelve, while a County Committee was appointed to run Cornwall, mindful as it was that Cornwall was still 'cavaleerish enough'.

At the Restoration in 1660 much of this was undone, with the Duchy and Stannary administrations put back in place. Thereafter, Cornwall was quiet, showing little inclination to join Puritan Somerset and Devon in the Monmouth rising of 1685, although in 1688 the imprisonment of Bishop Jonathan Trelawny in the Tower for refusing to read James II's 'Declaration of Indulgence' (which granted religious toleration to Catholics and Dissenters) caused some murmuring in Cornwall, expressed two centuries later in Robert Stephen Hawker's patriotic ballad 'The Song of the Western Men':

> And shall Trelawny live?
> Or shall Trelawny die?
> Here's twenty thousand Cornishmen
> Will know the reason why!

Perhaps surprisingly, the Cornish economy expanded during the Civil War and the subsequent Commonwealth. The populations of fishing ports such as Mevagissey and St Ives had grown markedly, reflecting the success of their fleets, while the tin mining industry had developed significantly, particularly in central and west Cornwall. Copper mining had also emerged towards the end of the 17th century, a prelude to the dominant role it would play in subsequent centuries.

# THE RETREAT OF THE
# CORNISH LANGUAGE

But if the Cornish economy had proved resilient in this period of turmoil, then the Cornish language was less so. During the Civil War Richard Symonds, a Royalist officer, had written that 'at Land's End they speak no English', while 'All beyond Truro they speak the Cornish language'. However, by 1662 the naturalist John Ray could report that even in St Just-in-Penwith in the far west 'We met none here but could speak English; few of the children could speak Cornish'. Perhaps as many as 22,000 could have spoken Cornish in 1600, a figure that declined to about 14,000 in 1650 and maybe as few as 5000 by 1700.

By 1750 very few speakers of this 'Late Cornish' (as it is known) were left, and by 1800 Cornish had all but disappeared as a spoken vernacular. Dolly Pentreath, the Mousehole fishwife who died in December 1777, is often said to have been 'the last Cornish speaker' but she was certainly survived by others with a knowledge of the language, such as William Bodinar who died in 1789 (he wrote that 'Cornish is all forgot with young people') and perhaps even John Davey of Boswednack, Zennor, who died in 1891 and was said to be able to converse in Cornish on a few simple subjects.

Dolly Pentreath
© Royal Institution of Cornwall

However, even as the language declined, there emerged a small group of enthusiasts determined to do what they could to keep it alive. Nicholas Boson of Newlyn, who had picked up the language as a child from his parents' servants, wrote his Nebbaz Gerriau dro tho Carnoack ('A Few Words about Cornish'), complaining that 'Our Cornish tongue hath been so long in the wane, that we can hardly hope to see it increase again', while from 1678 until his death in 1689 William Scawen of Molenick in the parish of St Germans devoted himself to Cornish. He listed the reasons for the language's decline, from the loss of contact with Brittany after the Reformation to the failure of people to correspond in Cornish or to preserve Cornish manuscripts. Other enthusiasts active at about this time included William Gwavas who, amongst other things, corresponded in Cornish with an unnamed contact in America, and William Tonkin who in about 1698 collected from one Edward Chirgwin a Cornish version of the well-known folk song 'Where are you going my pretty maid' ('Pela era why, moz, fettow, teag').

All this activity caught the attention of Edward Lhuyd, the Oxford scholar who had embarked upon a major comparative study of the Celtic languages. He visited Cornwall about 1700, finding that Cornish was still spoken in some 25 parishes from Land's End to the Lizard. He compared the language unfavourably to Welsh and Breton (it was now merely a peasant's tongue), considering it valid only as a curio for gentleman antiquarians, but he was sensitive enough to record the telling rhyme given to him by the parish clerk of St Just-in-Penwith:

*An lavar koth yw lavar gwir,*
*Na boz nevra doz vaz an tavaz re hir;*
*Bez den heb davaz a gollaz i dir.*

The old saying is a true saying,
A tongue too long never did good;
But the man with no tongue lost his land.

Mousehole

33

# THE 'BRITISH PROJECT'

This Victorian engraving shows how the Cornish (like the Irish) were falsely supposed to cause wrecks by showing lights which lured ships to their doom

In 1707 came the Act of Union of England and Scotland, creating the political entity of 'Great Britain' and re-inventing the 'British project' with a vengeance. Based on Protestantism and given unity of purpose by the wars with France, this new 'Britishness' prefigured Britain's maritime, commercial and imperial expansion. Like the 'sea-dogs' in the days of Elizabeth, the Cornish played their role to the full in this process. Falmouth emerged as an important port, home of the Packet service which from 1688-89 until 1850 carried the Post Office's mails to far-flung destinations the world over, from Spain and Portugal to the West Indies and South America.

Admiral Edward Boscawen, Lord Falmouth, born at Tregothnan in 1711, was typical of those Cornishmen whose service in the Royal Navy furthered the aims of the new 'Britishness'. Known variously as 'Wry-necked Dick' (because of an ugly scar) and 'Old Dreadnought' (after one of his warships), Boscawen was fiercely Cornish, giving preference to Cornish officers and creating what his critics like to call a little Cornish navy of his own. He fought in numerous actions, including that off Lagos in 1759 in which he managed to disperse a French fleet, with many enemy ships captured or destroyed. But he was also known for his concern for the welfare of his men, improving their diet and introducing new standards of hygiene in his ships. William Bligh, from St Tudy, was another Cornishman who rose to the rank of Admiral, and he is remembered today for the famous mutiny on the Bounty but also for a second mutiny when he was Governor of New South Wales and was deposed by the unscrupulous officers of the so-called 'Rum Corps' who controlled the colony's economy.

And yet, while such Cornishmen were embroiled across the globe in the affairs of British expansion, for many people closer to home Cornwall remained a forbidding and distant land, a 'West Barbary' where (according to one visitor in 1775) the people were 'very strange kind of beings, half savages at best... as rough as bears, selfish as swine, obstinate as mules, and as hard as the native iron'. Even in 1851 Wilkie Collins, the novelist, could write that the Cornish were 'other' and that Cornwall was 'a county where, it must be remembered, a stranger is doubly a stranger' and where, he said, 'the national feeling is almost entirely merged in the local feeling; where a man speaks of himself as Cornish in much the same way that a Welshman speaks of himself as Welsh'.

Engraving of Tintagel Castle

Food riots, often perpetrated by the much-feared tinners, were commonplace throughout the eighteenth and early nineteenth centuries, especially in times of shortage, and did much to colour Cornwall's reputation as 'a dismal country'.

Although there is no evidence of Cornish folk deliberately luring ships to their dooms, the Cornish were well-known as 'wreckers', routinely plundering those vessels that had had the misfortune to come to grief on Cornwall's treacherous coasts:

> The Eliza of Liverpool came on shore
> To feed the hungry and clothe the poor.

Smuggling too added to Cornwall's unsavoury reputation, an activity that has acquired retrospectively an aura of high romance but which in those days was a dangerous and often violent way to make a living. Many were the struggles between desperate bands of smugglers and the Preventive (Customs) officers, as in December 1802 when the smuggling smack **Vigilant** was intercepted off Polperro by a Preventive cutter.

The **Vigilant** refused to heave-to, and the cutter fired a shot into her rigging to disable her, resulting in the unintentional but hardly surprising deaths of two of the smuggling party. Even the law-abiding activity of fishing could be dangerous off the Cornish coasts, this precarious livelihood prompting various taboos that became enmeshed in Cornish folklore. White hares were thought to be unlucky, and so too were clergymen if spotted near a boat that was preparing for sea. Pilchards were the mainstay of the Cornish fishing industry from the seventeenth century until well into the nineteenth, with much of the demand coming from the Roman Catholic countries of the Mediterranean. As a Cornish rhyme put it:

> Here's health to the Pope
> And may he repent
> And lengthen six months
> The term of his Lent.
> It's always declared
> Betwixt the two poles
> There's nothing like pilchards
> For saving of souls.

When pilchards arrived in huge shoals on the coast, everyone in the town or village rushed to the boats in a massive communal effort to take as many as possible

© Royal Institution of Cornwall

# MINERS
# AND INVENTORS

The two 'Crowns' engine houses of Botallack mine, where the shafts extended out below the sea

Although fishing was important to the eighteenth and 19th century Cornish economy, it was mining that dominated. As early as the 1680s there had been a number of important copper mines in the Redruth district and by the mid 18th century famous mines such as Wheal Busy, Roskear, Dolcoath and Cook's Kitchen were already prominent amongst Cornwall's copper producers. Gwennap parish emerged as 'the richest square mile on earth', and when Wheal Virgin was opened there in 1757 it was said that it had yielded copper to the value of £5700 in its first two weeks of operation. By 1810 Cornish copper mining began to move beyond its Gwennap and Camborne-Redruth heartland, eastwards to the area around St Austell Bay (mines such as Crinnis and Fowey Consols) and westwards to St Just-in-Penwith where mines such as Levant clung literally to the Atlantic-battered cliffs and were worked out under the sea. In 1836 there was a significant discovery of copper on Caradon Hill, on the southern slopes of Bodmin Moor, leading swiftly to the development of new mines in the St Cleer district, while in the 1840s there were further copper finds in the Tamar valley – on the Cornish side around Calstock and Gunnislake but on the Devon bank of the river too.

Although copper was the chief Cornish mineral, tin mining was also significant, as indeed it had been for centuries. By 1800 demand for tin plate in the British domestic market was rising rapidly, leading to the development of Great Wheal Vor and a number of other tin mines in the neighbourhood of Helston and Marazion as well as at St Just-in-Penwith where workings such as Wheal Spearne and Carnyorth Moor were in full swing by 1815.

There were later tin booms in 1850-64 and 1870-72, the latter leading to the rise of a string of important mines along the Great Flat Lode south of Carn Brea, near Redruth, and to the development of Wheal Owles and other mines on the cliffs at St Just. From the late 1830s onwards a number of Camborne-Redruth copper mines had also turned to tin extraction, tin having been found at depth, a change that helped them weather the crash of Cornish copper in 1866. Iron and other minerals were also mined in Cornwall but of particular importance was lead, worked at East Wheal Rose at Newlyn East and further east around Menheniot and Herodsfoot.

Hand in hand with deep mining went the development of steam engineering in Cornwall. Early Newcomen and Watt engines had been erected on Cornish mines in the 18th century but when James Watt's patents expired in 1800 a new generation of Cornish engineers and inventors – Richard Trevithick, Arthur Woolf, Samuel Grose, William Sims and many more – arose to develop and perfect what became known as the Cornish beam engine.

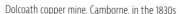
Dolcoath copper mine, Camborne, in the 1830s

Used for winding, pumping and stamping (ore crushing) as well as in the larger mines for operating 'man engines' to enable miners to ride to surface or underground, these versatile machines were constructed in foundries across Cornwall. Some famous foundries included William West's at St Blazey, the Perran Foundry at Perran-ar-worthal, and Harvey & Co of Hayle. Copper was smelted in South Wales, with a two-way trade between Cornish and Welsh ports handling the export from Cornwall of copper ore and the import of coal, while a system of mineral railways was developed to link Cornish mines and harbours. Tin, however, was smelted in Cornwall, leading to the establishment of smelting works in centres such as Redruth, Penzance and Truro.

Alongside the new generation of engineers emerged great entrepreneurial families and individuals such as the Lemons, the Williams family, the Bassets of Tehidy, the Fox family of Falmouth, and JTTreffry, 'The King of Mid Cornwall', who put their energies and money into Cornish mining and prospered as a result. Important too were the scientists, such as Sir Humphry Davy (inventor of the miner's safety lamp and a President of the Royal Society) and the astronomer Jonathan Couch Adams (who discovered the planet Neptune), while the establishment in the early nineteenth century of prestigious learned societies such as the Royal Institution of Cornwall, the Royal Cornwall Polytechnic Society and the Royal Geological Society of Cornwall emphasised the position of Cornwall at the forefront of technological advance.

This is a replica of the world's very first full-size self-propelled vehicle, which was constructed by Richard Trevithick in 1800 – nearly 30 years before Stephenson's Rocket. It was the ancestor of every steam locomotive and arguably of every road vehicle too, and it is a symbol of the time when Cornwall led the world in developing new technologies

Copper and tin mine,
Botallack St Just, Cornwall 1869

# METHODISM
# AND RADICALISM

Indeed, this all-pervading sense of industrial prowess underpinned the Cornish identity as it re-invented itself in the late eighteenth and nineteenth centuries. Mining was Cornwall and Cornwall was mining, and Cornish people were fiercely proud of their reputation as the world's greatest hardrock miners, nurturing a sense of difference that still insisted that England did not begin until one crossed the Tamar.

To this identity was wedded a distinctly Cornish brand of Methodism. John Wesley had made frequent visits to Cornwall in the second half of the 18th century, and in 1781, at the age of 78 years, could still attract a congregation of some 20,000 people when he preached at Gwennap Pit.

The Bible Christians were especially associated with Cornwall but other denominations, including the Primitive Methodists and the Methodist New Connexion, as well as the Wesleyans themselves, made a major contribution to Cornish society. The Methodists encouraged 'self-help' and 'mutual improvement', and they also influenced the Liberal Party as it developed in 19th century Cornwall, helping to mould a particular kind of Cornish religious and political radicalism.

Gwennap Pit today

© Gwennap Pit

Every Whit Monday massive crowds of Cornish Methodists gathered at Gwennap Pit. This had been one of the Wesleys' favourite preaching places

# EMIGRATION

Captain Alexander Pope – far left, sitting – with a group of Cornish miners in South Africa in 1896

© Royal Institution of Cornwall

One early consequence of this emerging radicalism was an enthusiasm for emigration, first apparent during the repressive days after the end of the Napoloeonic Wars in 1815, when many Cornish folk began to look overseas for opportunities for social and economic mobility and for religious freedom, not least release from the tithes that had to be paid to the Church of England.

Many of the first emigrants were from the Bible Christian, farming districts of North Cornwall; they sailed from Padstow and other Cornish ports to establish new agricultural communities in North America. By the 1820s they were joined by miners anxious to earn the high wages that awaited their skills in the developing silver, gold and copper mines of Latin America. These 'Cousin Jacks' (as they were known) asserted their superiority above all other classes of miners.

Often the miners went alone, sending 'homepay' to support relatives at home, but sometimes they took their wives (the 'Cousin Jennies') and families to start new lives abroad.

In the 1830s and 1840s lead and copper finds attracted Cornish emigrants to Wisconsin and Michigan in the United States, and in the mid-1840s – the so-called 'Hungry Forties' in Cornwall when the potato crop failed and many almost starved – copper discoveries at Kapunda and Burra Burra drew thousands of Cornish people to South Australia.

In 1849 the Cornish were involved in the Californian Gold Rush, as they were in Victoria in Australia in 1851, putting such names as Grass Valley (California) and Ballarat (Victoria) firmly on the Cornish mining map of the world.

Between 1859-1861 there were new copper strikes at Wallaroo and Moonta in South Australia, in a district soon known as 'Australia's Little Cornwall', and when Cornwall's copper industry suddenly collapsed in 1866, further waves of Cornish emigrants left for destinations in America, Australia, New Zealand and elsewhere. By the late 19th century, South Africa's gold and diamond fields had become a familiar home for the emigrant Cornish, with many thousands of pounds being sent home annually to support families in what was now a severely depressed Cornish economy.

Trevaunance Cove, St Agnes, on 20th July 1910

Trevaunance Cove, St Agnes at present

The crash of Cornish copper was followed by the gradual but erratic decline of tin, and after the First World War, as emigration dried up, so unemployment and poverty were felt keenly. Although the expansion of the china clay industry did something to fill the economic gap left by mining, some Cornish people, including the writer Sir Arthur Quiller Couch, argued that Cornwall should now turn its hand more fully to tourism.

A rash of grand hotels began to appear on the Cornish cliffs in the 1890s. Many, like this one at Newquay, were designed by the Cornish architect Silvanus Trevai

Artists such as Stanhope Forbes and others of the Newlyn School had already been attracted by Cornwall's sense of 'difference', and the Great Western Railway invented the 'Cornish Riviera', inviting tourists from other parts of Britain to visit what it portrayed as an exotic, foreign clime, 'a Duchy that is in every respect un-English'.

# THE CORNISH REVIVALISTS

The idea of Cornwall as a Celtic nation was also advocated by the Cornish Revivalists, a movement which strove to revive the Cornish language and to promote Cornish traditions. Henry Jenner published his 'A Handbook of the Cornish Language' in 1904, the same year that the Great Western Railway introduced its 'Cornish Riviera Limited' express train, and in the inter-war period Robert Morton Nance worked hard to produce what he called 'Unified' Cornish, a synthesis based largely on the Middle Cornish texts of the medieval period.

In 1928 a Cornish Gorsedd, based on those of Wales and Brittany, was set up, a college of bards which sought to promote the language and culture of Cornwall.

After the Second World War, the Revivalist movement acquired a political dimension, leading to the foundation in 1951 of Mebyon Kernow (Sons of Cornwall), a political party which called for self-government for Cornwall. Although Mebyon Kernow has never won any Westminster seats, it has been more successful at local levels and has influenced the thinking of other political parties active in Cornwall, particularly the Liberal Democrats. Although many people have moved into Cornwall from other parts of Britain in the decades since 1960, Cornwall has remained an area of high unemployment and relative poverty and poor housing, in marked contrast to neighbouring southern England.

In more positive ways Cornwall has also remained 'different', a more self-confident assertion of Cornish identity leading to further growth in the language movement (though by the late 1980s it had split into three competing factions) and expressed in the widespread flying of the St Piran's Cross, the Cornish flag, including at County Hall in Truro.

Novelists and poets, whether indigenous like Jack Clemo, DM Thomas, Charles Causley and Janie Bolitho or 'incomers' such as Daphne du Maurier, Winston Graham, Sir John Betjeman and Patrick Gate, also projected a particular 'Cornishness'. When, in recent years, the Cornwall rugby team has performed well in the County Championship (which it has won on several occasions), it has received the passionate support of 'Trelawny's Army', the many thousands of Cornish fans who march to Twickenham bedecked in the traditional Cornish colours of black-and-gold.

By the late 1990s Cornwall had been recognised as a region by the European Union and given so-called 'Objective One' status, in so doing unlocking millions of pounds of potential funding and helping to create a new mood of optimism in Cornwall's business community. The 'In Pursuit of Excellence' initiative, which drew together business people and other community leaders, encouraged and drew attention to the multiplicity of new, 'high-tech' companies in Cornwall producing high-quality products for the global market, while others identified Cornwall's distinctive identity and special maritime location as key strengths to be deployed in future economic development.

Calls for a Cornish university were met by a Combined Universities in Cornwall campus at Tremough, near Penryn, a joint venture by the University of Exeter and University College Falmouth University. In 2001, following the establishment of the Scottish Parliament and Assemblies in Wales and Northern Ireland, a Cornish petition of more than 50,000 signatures demanded a similar devolutionary Assembly for Cornwall. In 2009 Cornwall County Council was replaced by a new unitary 'Cornwall Council', perhaps the first step on the road to a Cornish Assembly.

Levant Mine
© Sean Gibson

Cornwall's separate identity was also strengthened by the 'official' recognition of the Cornish language by the British government in 2002 under the terms of the Council of Europe Charter on Regional and Minority Languages. In 2006 there was further good news, when the Cornish mining landscapes of Cornwall and West Devon were awarded UNESCO World Heritage Site status, fitting acknowledgement of the global significance of Cornwall's industrial heritage. Equally important was the granting of 'national minority' status to the Cornish people themselves in 2014, affording them recognition alongside the Welsh, Scots and Northern Irish under the Council of Europe Convention for the Protection of National Minorities.

Eden Project

Meanwhile, institutions such as the Tate St Ives, the Hall for Cornwall, and the Eden Project had achieved popular acclaim throughout Britain and beyond for their contributions to culture, the arts and the environment. Kneehigh Theatre, described by Cornish poet Charles Causley as 'truly Cornwall's National Theatre', had won similar recognition for performances across the UK of plays such as 'Tristan and Yseult' (based on the Cornish legend) and Nick Darke's 'The King of Prussia' (about a famous Cornish smuggler). New plays by Cornish playwright Alan M. Kent were similarly popular, among them 'Surfing Tommies', 'The Tin Violin', and 'Oogly es Sin: The Lamentable Ballad of Anthony Payne, Cornish Giant'. Much voluntary effort was expended in achieving this high level of creative and artistic activity in Cornwall, as people gave willingly of their time and enthusiasm, and the voluntary sector was also responsible for supporting important Cornish charities, from the Air Ambulance (Britain's first) to the international disaster relief charity Shelterbox, founded in Helston in 2000.

© Ron Westwater

GWR current upgrade of the main line service and rolling stock is further evidence of investment into Cornwall

These positive initiatives appeared to culminate in the devolution of key administrative powers – from transport spending to health care management – to Cornwall Council in 2015, in what the press dubbed 'DevoKernow'. However, as critics were swift to point out, real power in crucial areas such as planning and housing was retained firmly at Westminster, preventing Cornwall Council from intervening effectively to shape Cornish development policies. By now, Cornwall was seemingly in the grip of a determined developer-led strategy, which meant thousands more houses and a spiralling population. Local infrastructure, from schools to GP surgeries, was placed under enormous pressure, while second-homes and high prices excluded many local people from the housing market. Many felt that Cornwall's environmental and economic sustainability was now under threat as never before, creating a new mood of anxiety and uncertainty.

In June 2016 the majority of people in Cornwall (56%) voted in the referendum to leave the Economic Union. Although 16 billion pounds had been poured into Cornwall by the EU in the preceding fifteen years, funding a multiplicity of projects such as the Penryn university campus, the provision of super-fast broadband, and improvements to the Cornish rail network, many people – especially the elderly and the least well-off – felt that they had been 'left behind' and had not benefitted from this investment. But at a stroke Cornwall's hard-won regional status was repudiated, with the prospect of losing the additional 400 million pounds of European funding earmarked for the period to 2020. 'Brexit' fears added to concerns about the future of the Cornish economy, and of the ability of Cornwall itself –despite all the progress of recent years – to sustain its separate identity in the face of a relentless 'development' which merely promised more houses, more roads, more cars, more people, and the loss of a distinctive landscape under concrete and bitumen. Would Cornwall continue to remain a land apart?